jE MCG
McGuire, Leslie.
Big Dan's moving van

BIG DAN'S MOVING VAN

A Random House PICTUREBACK®

BIG DAN'S

Library of Congress Cataloging-in-Publication Data: McGuire, Leslie. Big Dan's moving van / by Leslie McGuire ; illustrated by Joe Mathieu. p. cm. – (A Random House pictureback) Summary: Big Dan and his moving van move all the possessions of the Moore family to their new home in California. ISBN 0-679-80565-6 (pbk.) [1. Moving, Household—Fiction.] I. Mathieu, Joseph, ill. II. Title PZ7. M4786B1 1993 [E]—dc20   90-44173
Manufactured in the United States of America 10 9 8 7 6 5 4 3 2

MOVING VAN

By Leslie McGuire
Illustrated by Joe Mathieu

Random House 🏠 **New York**

Big Dan drives a moving van. He helps people move from their old house to their new house. That's a lot of work.

First thing in the morning, Big Dan goes to the moving company to pick up his van. The dispatcher tells him his assignment is to move the Moores from New York to California.

Big Dan's moving van is a big tractor-trailer. Big Dan puts his supplies in the trailer. He needs boxes, pads, straps, hand trucks, and dollies. He checks to make sure the ramp on the back of the truck is working properly and can be raised and lowered.

Then Big Dan and his helpers climb into the cab. They are ready to go.

Big Dan drives to the Moores' house. The whole family is waiting outside.

Michael and Kathy watch as Big Dan takes his supplies out of the van. Big Dan tells them that even though California is three thousand miles away, he will make sure all their things get to their new house safely.

Big Dan carries the boxes into the house.

First he carefully packs all the things that are breakable. He wraps the dishes and vases in newspaper before he puts them in boxes.

Then Big Dan and his helpers pack the clothes and toys and books.

When each box is filled, Big Dan tapes it shut and numbers it. Then he writes the number on his list. Big Dan has to make a list of everything that is going in the van.

His helpers wheel the boxes out to the van on a hand truck and stack them inside.

After all the boxes are in the van, it is time to load the furniture. Big Dan takes the bunk beds apart before he carries them out. He wraps pads around the tables to protect them. His helpers bring out the couch on a dolly.

Everything is strapped inside the van. Nothing must fall or bounce or shake loose when the van goes over a bump or around a corner.

By afternoon everything that was inside the house is now inside Big Dan's moving van—except the lampshades. Big Dan puts all the lampshades in the Moores' car so they won't get crushed. Then he drives the car right up the ramp and puts it in the moving van too!

Big Dan closes the van doors and locks them tight.
He waves good-bye to the Moores. The Moores are going
to fly to California. A taxi will take them to the airport.

Big Dan drives to the moving company and drops off his helpers. Then he gets on the highway and heads west.

Big Dan stops at the weigh station in New Jersey. He drives onto the scale. He knows how much his van weighs when it is empty. The scale tells him how much the van weighs now that it is full.

Big Dan calls his dispatcher and tells him how many pounds of furniture are on the van. He also says there is a little extra space left on his van. The dispatcher asks him to stop in Ohio on his way to California and make a pickup.

Big Dan writes down two addresses—the address where he must make the pickup...and the address where he must make the delivery.

Big Dan drives on until he gets hungry. He eats dinner at a truck stop in Pennsylvania. He talks to the other truck drivers there. Then he lies down in the back of his cab for a good night's sleep. Big Dan is tired.

Big Dan gets up early and eats a big breakfast. He fills the gas tank and gets back on the highway.

Big Dan's next stop is the Walkers' house in Ohio. The Walkers are sending a beautiful rocking horse to their granddaughter. Big Dan covers the rocking horse with pads and puts it into the van.

Then Big Dan waves to the Walkers and drives off.

Late that afternoon Big Dan arrives in Illinois. He stops in front of the apartment house where the Walkers' granddaughter lives.

He takes the rocking horse up to the fourth floor in the elevator. The Walkers' daughter signs the receipt.

Big Dan still has a long way to go. He drives through many states— Missouri, Kansas, Colorado, Utah, and Nevada. It takes him five more days before he reaches California!

Big Dan stops to call his dispatcher. He says he'll be at the Moores' new house at eight o'clock the next morning. The dispatcher lets the Moores know, then calls to arrange for two helpers to work with Big Dan.

In the morning Big Dan picks up his two helpers. They drive to the Moores' new house. The whole family is waiting on the front lawn.

The Moores are very glad to see their furniture arrive. Mrs. Moore gives Big Dan a check to pay for the move.

Now it's time to unload. First, Big Dan drives the car—full of lampshades—off the van. The car has just gone 3,000 miles without using any gas at all!

Then Big Dan and his helpers begin to unload the
Moores' furniture. Big Dan makes check marks on his list
as each piece of furniture is taken off the van.

The Moores tell Big Dan where to put everything. One bunk bed goes in Michael's new bedroom. One bunk bed goes in Kathy's new bedroom. The couch goes in the living room. The dishes go in the kitchen.

Soon Michael and Kathy's new house begins to look just like home.

At last everything is done. Big Dan packs up his
supplies and says good-bye to the Moores. Even though he
is tired, Big Dan feels good. It has been a successful move.

Then Big Dan climbs into his van and drives away.

Big Dan drops off his helpers and gets into the back of his cab. He needs a good night's sleep. Tomorrow he has to pick up another load of furniture. His new assignment is to move the Coopers from California to New York.

After Big Dan moves the Coopers to New York, he brings his van back to the moving company. The mechanics in the garage will get it ready for the next long drive.

Then Big Dan goes home to his own house, where he can eat in his own kitchen and sleep in his own bed. It's good to rest after all that work!